THE TURTLE AND THE UNIVERSE

DATE DUE

DEMCO 38-297

THE TURTLE

AND THE

UNIVERSE

STEPHEN WHITT

Illustrated by Stephanie Hernandez

Prometheus Books

59 John Glenn Drive
Amherst, New York 14228–2119

Published 2008 by Prometheus Books

Inquiries should be addressed to
Prometheus Books
59 John Glenn Drive
Amherst, New York 14228–2119
VOICE: 716–691–0133, ext. 210
FAX: 716–691–0137
WWW.PROMETHEUSBOOKS.COM

12 11 10 09 08   5 4 3 2 1

Library of Congress Cataloging-in-Publication Data

Whitt, Stephen, 1968–
    The turtle and the universe / by Stephen Whitt.
        p. cm.
    ISBN 978–1–59102–626–6 (pbk.)
    1. Sea turtles—Juvenile literature. 2. Life—Origin—Juvenile literature.
3. Cosmogony—Juvenile literature. I. Title.

QL666.C536W53 2008
597.92'8—dc22

                                                            2008018167

Printed in the United States of America on acid-free paper

To Julie,
who always believed

INTRODUCTION

How did we get here? Where are we going? What *is* the universe, anyway?

This is a book about asking big questions.

There are many such books, written by famous scientists and deep thinkers. This book is different, because the questions come by way of a group of creatures that, so far as we know, has never asked them before.

They were here long before us, and they may outlast us still. They are the sea turtles—ocean travelers, deep-sea divers, and builders in sand. They are long-lived and methodical creatures, driven by habit and instinct. They seem (to us, at least) to be unconcerned with the big questions of life. Instead, they are content to simply be. And yet the cycles of their lives—a frantic emergence at the edge of the ocean, arduous journeys across

vast distances, and finally a return home, often from very far away, to sand they have not touched since their first days of life—speak to us of the wonder, the mystery, the poetry to be found in this exquisite and surprising universe.

In this book, we will follow the journey of one member of this ancient assemblage, a female sea turtle returning home to lay her eggs. We will witness her in her natural environment, as peaceful and graceful a swimmer as our planet has ever produced. We will watch her emerge from the surf to begin a perilous crawl up a moonlit beach. And we will see her abandon her own precious eggs on that beach, leaving them to the uncertain care of the sand—sand from which she herself was born.

As we consider the journey of the sea turtle, we will not shy away from the fact of evolution—both of the sea turtle and of the universe surrounding her. That the sea turtle—an ocean creature that breathes air and lays her eggs on land—must have evolved is clear. To really know the sea turtle, to understand where she came from, where she is going, and why she is the way she is, we are compelled to travel deep into the past to learn the hidden history of the turtle, her planet, and the universe itself.

We will see how the elements that make up a turtle were first formed long ago in the center of a giant, dying star. We will witness the birth of the Moon, of the mountains, and of the sand that gave the turtle life. We will see how the turtle's ancestors changed over time, and we will discover how one surprising source of those changes takes us back to the stars. And finally we will explore the turtle's eventual fate, a fate we also may share. It is a story of wonder; of time and energy, beginnings and endings, life, death, and rebirth. I hope you enjoy the trip.

CHAPTER ONE

The turtle swims slowly, her low, domed shell quietly breaking the dark surface of the placid sea. Overhead, stars sprinkle the sky with their cold light, but the turtle, whose eyes have evolved for the ocean she calls home, could not see the stars even if she looked straight up. No matter, for tonight her attention is elsewhere.

Within the turtle, chemical factories churn. Oxygen gulped from the sky combines with sea grass devoured earlier in the day. The energy of sunlight, stored in the plant's cells, is released within the turtle, a slow burn that fuels the turtle's every thought and movement. Ultimately, the turtle is powered by sunshine.

Each of the turtle's cells is a wonder, a chemical machine that makes the turtle go. All this chemistry in all these cells—muscle cells, skin cells, liver cells, heart cells—is the chemistry of the element carbon. The most versatile element in the universe, carbon is the key to our kind of life. Its long chains of molecules are ideal for building the complex structures found in turtles, and in all the other living things we know.

The turtle's brain, an intricate and complex carbon machine itself, coordinates the contractions of the turtle's powerful shoulder muscles, directing movements that push seawater down and back, propelling her along as gracefully as any bird of prey.

Deep within her rigid shell, the turtle's heart beats forty times a minute. The low, slow, churning three-chambered pump has changed little since the turtle's fishlike ancestors first crawled from the sea to make the land their home. It is in the ocean that the turtle's most distant ancestors first arose. It is to that ocean that the sea turtle has fully returned—with two crucial exceptions. First, she must breathe air, and she must return to land to lay her eggs. The turtle encounters the first of these legacies each time she lifts her head from the water to fill her lungs. On this journey, the most difficult and dangerous of her adult life, the turtle will confront the second exception to her ancient watery ways.

STAR MOTHER

Why are there sea turtles? There are many ways to answer this question. Sea turtles are survivors. They're tough. They're very good at making little sea turtles. But one deeper answer must be this: there are sea turtles because there are stars. To find out what that means, we must journey deep inside a star, for sea turtles are built from the elements that make up the universe, and, with a few important exceptions, these elements are born inside stars.

In this first part of our journey, we will witness the birth of an element called carbon. Carbon will prove to be not only the most indispensable element in the turtle's body but also the key to all the elements to follow. Without carbon, the universe we know could not be.

Elements are the building blocks that make up the universe. Many common substances are not elements, but instead are made of two or more elements combined together through chemistry. You may know that water, for instance, is made of the elements hydrogen (H) and oxygen (O), forming a compound called water (H_2O).

The "2" in H_2O means that for every one bit of oxygen there are two bits of hydrogen. Today we call those bits atoms. An atom is the smallest possible bit of an element. But one of the remarkable discoveries of science is that atoms themselves are made of still smaller pieces.

THE SIMPLEST ATOM

Hydrogen atoms are the most common atoms in stars. Hydrogen is not only the most abundant element in the universe, it is also the simplest. Inside a star, most hydrogen atoms are reduced to a single piece, a tiny bit of matter called a proton. The proton forms the tiny, dense center or nucleus of the atom. We call this kind of atom hydrogen-1 (often written as ^1H).

As you might guess, if there's a hydrogen-1, there's also a hydrogen-2 (or ^2H). The inside of a star is so hot (around fifteen million degrees or hotter), the atoms there zip about at fantastic speed and very often collide with one another. On rare occasions, when two hydrogen-1 atoms (two protons) collide, they may stick.

The two protons can only stick, though, if one of them changes into a different bit of matter called a neutron. When this happens a new atom called hydrogen-2 (or ^2H) is formed, with one proton and one neutron in the nucleus. Another name for ^2H is deuterium.

The change from ^1H to ^2H is called a nuclear reaction. The new nucleus is different in many ways from the nucleus of the ^1H atom. Most important, ^2H is just about (though not exactly) twice as massive as ^1H. But ^2H is still hydrogen.

SOMETHING NEW INSIDE THE SUN

If we add two more protons to ^2H, something very different happens. As before, one of these two new protons must change into a neutron. The resulting atom has four pieces: two protons—one from the ^2H atom, plus the one *unchanged* proton—and two neutrons—one from the ^2H atom, plus the one *changed* proton. But the new atom isn't ^4H (in fact, there's no such thing as ^4H).

The number of protons in an atom is important in a surprising way. Change the number of protons, and you've created a different element. Adding neutrons (like changing ^1H to ^2H) doesn't change the element, but adding protons does. So this new atom, with two protons and two neutrons, is no longer hydrogen. Instead, it is an element called helium or, to be more exact, helium-4 (written as ^4He).

Now comes the magic part. Four ^1H atoms went into making the single ^4He atom. But a single ^4He atom is a tiny bit less massive than four ^1H atoms all by themselves. Inside a star that tiny missing mass doesn't disappear, but instead changes into energy. It is the energy released in this nuclear reaction, multiplied over and over again inside a star, that makes the star shine. Sunshine and starshine are the direct result of hydrogen turning into helium. Starlight is made by atoms.

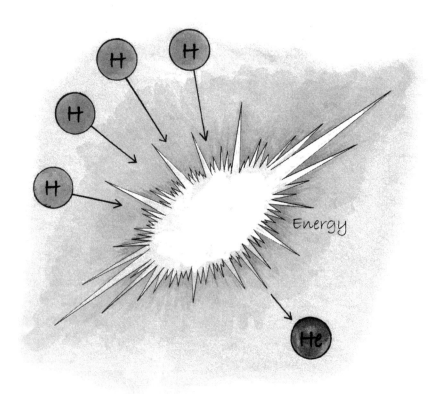

ASH TO FUEL

While you're digesting that big idea, here comes the next one. Stars can't last forever. Eventually the hydrogen near the center of the star runs low; then what? The answer to this question leads, in time, to all the beauty and wonder of the world around you, including the ancient way of the sea turtle.

A star is a balancing act. Stars have so much mass that their own gravitational attraction is gigantic.

Without something to push out against the inward pull of their own gravity, stars would squish themselves into a tiny fraction of their original size. For most of a star's life, the outward push comes from the energy of hydrogen turning into helium.

When the hydrogen near the center of the star runs short, that outward push diminishes slightly, and the inside of the star starts to shrink and heat up. At about one hundred million degrees, the second stage of the star's life begins. Helium-4 atoms collide with one another so forcefully at this temperature that they stick, creating something new yet again. This new atom, with four protons and four neutrons, is called beryllium-8 (^{8}Be). But there's a problem.

Beryllium-8 is unstable, blowing itself apart in a tiny fraction of a second. Inside a very hot, contracting star, however, so many helium atoms are colliding every moment that there is always some ^{8}Be available. Occasionally, a third ^{4}He atom will pass very near a newly formed ^{8}Be atom before the atom has time to self-destruct. When ^{8}Be and ^{4}He stick together, they form yet another new atom. This atom has six protons and six neutrons and is called carbon-12 (written as ^{12}C).

We are now one giant step closer to the sea turtle, for carbon-12 is not only stable, it is also the key to all life on Earth. Without this tendency of beryllium and helium to form ^{12}C inside stars, there would be almost no carbon (and, as we shall see, almost no other elements beyond carbon) in the universe. It is this knife-edge process—the transformation of helium atoms, through unstable beryllium-8, into stable carbon-12—that is the ultimate source of trees, butterflies, and sea turtles. The stuff of sea turtles is built within the stars.

CHAPTER TWO

*T*he turtle swims in a sea of chemicals. Many are vital to her life. In the seawater surrounding her and in the plants and animals she consumes are all the elements she needs to survive—calcium for her shell and bones, iron for her blood, magnesium for her brain tissue, and dozens more. There are also heavier elements in the water, including more gold than can be found in all the world's banks, yet dissolved in so fine a state that its recovery remains (thankfully) impractical.

Far below the turtle lies the dark ocean floor. In some places, water seeps through cracks in the ocean's crust, where sizzling-hot rocks superheat the water. The water picks up a deadly brew of chemicals and is then ejected, black and billowing, back into the open water through vents and underwater volcanoes. In this world, hostile and alien to our surface-loving eyes, we might expect to find

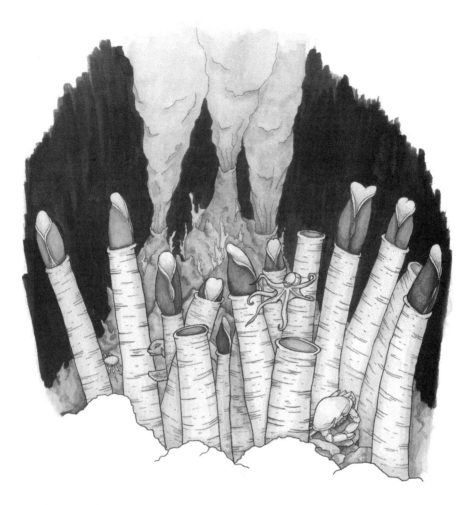

nothing alive. Yet somehow these places, the hot hydro-thermal vents of our planet's ocean floor, support a garden of living creatures.

Two-foot-long tube worms, animals with neither mouth nor gut, gather food from foul-smelling water poisoned with hydrogen sulfide (the gas that makes rotten eggs smell bad). Alongside the worms are ghostly white crabs, scuttling about just inches away from water so hot it would boil them in their shells. Some worms survive on the margins, their front ends in water hot enough to roast, their tail ends in water cold enough to freeze. And everywhere in this world there are bacteria—tiny, single-celled creatures that drive the entire ecosystem by harvesting energy from the hot chemical stew. These bacteria play the same role in their ecosystem as the sunlight-gathering green plants play far above. Unlike life at the surface, this community lives not on energy from the Sun, but instead draws on energy from a different and far more ancient source.

LIVING AND DYING

In chapter 1 we saw how the carbon making up a turtle is born inside stars. In fact, the creation of carbon is key to the formation of all the other elements to follow. But how do carbon and the other elements make the journey from star to sea turtle? How do turtles emerge from stars?

In this part of our story we will come closer still to the sea turtle by witnessing the lives and deaths of the stars themselves. The largest of these stars, whose violent deaths are among the most spectacular events in the universe, will surprise us with a gift that proves indispensable to the sea turtle, and to many other creatures as well.

Let's return to our aging star in which helium is changing into carbon. While this process goes on, the star endures other changes. Pressure from within causes the outer part of the star to expand and cool, even as the interior of the star heats and shrinks. The expanding star slowly becomes a cooler, redder, hugely swollen version of itself called a red giant.

Near the center of the red giant star, helium eventually grows scarce—just as hydrogen grew scarce earlier in the star's life cycle. For a star around the mass of the Sun, this helium crisis signals the beginning of the end of the star's energy-producing nuclear reactions. Some of the remaining helium will fuse with the newly formed carbon atoms to produce another familiar and important atom, oxygen. But for a star about the mass of the Sun, atom building goes no further.

For a more massive star, the higher temperatures near the star's center—as high as a billion degrees for the most massive stars—drive the creation of more complex elements. As the temperature rises, atoms fly about at higher and higher speeds. Carbon fuses with helium to form oxygen, oxygen fuses with helium to produce neon, magnesium, silicon, calcium, and others. Each nuclear reaction releases energy, but each reaction produces less energy than the one that came before. The star is dying.

As it contracts and expands with changing temperature, the star blows off its outer layers as huge clouds of gas. This gas may include some of the new elements forged inside the aging star, including carbon, oxygen, and their children. The new elements drift about in the great empty spaces between the stars, enriching the wispy clouds of gas they find there. One day, perhaps, these elements will be swept up into a swirling storm of dust and gas that slowly forms into a new star and its planets. The universe evolves from itself.

Eventually, the red giant's internal temperature drops so low that it can no longer support energy-releasing nuclear reactions. If the star is about the mass of the Sun, it will shrink into a small, hot, incredibly dense star known as a white dwarf. The white dwarf will slowly cool and darken, a quiet, almost peaceful death.

BRIGHTER THAN A HUNDRED BILLION SUNS

For stars much more massive than the Sun, a very different end awaits. Within these stars, energy-releasing nuclear reactions continue until the stars produce an element called iron. Building elements beyond iron does not release energy, but instead absorbs it. Iron marks the end of useful nuclear reactions within stars. Yet there is still another energy source that stars may call upon. That energy source is gravity.

Remember that stars are balancing acts. When a

truly massive star runs out of useful nuclear fuel, it collapses right through the iron barrier. The force of gravity, no longer held back by nuclear fire, shrinks the star's core smaller and smaller until the core rebounds in a gigantic explosion called a supernova. In this violent explosion, so much light is produced that the star

may for a while outshine its entire galaxy of hundreds of billions of ordinary stars. And, crucially for our story, suddenly there's a lot of extra energy available to build new kinds of atoms.

Elements more complex than iron, including lead, bismuth, and gold, are produced only very slowly in a living giant star. But in its supernova death, the star forms these elements in an instant and ejects them deep into space. All the gold in the universe is built in these massive stars, most of it formed in the star's final gasp. All the gold in all the banks of our world is nothing more (and nothing less!) than the multibillion-year-old ash of long-dead giant stars.

Other elements are formed only in supernova explosions themselves. These elements have names like thorium, polonium, and uranium, and they possess an astonishing property. The atoms of these elements store within themselves the energy of the explosion that formed them. Some atoms might hold onto this star energy for billions of years before releasing it in their own mini-explosions. We call these atoms radioactive.

ATOMS OUT OF BALANCE

Radioactive atoms are unstable. It is almost as if the exploding star that created them got a bit carried away, creating atoms so big or so unbalanced in their number of neutrons and protons that they simply can't last. Some of these atoms survive for only seconds. Others may last ten billion years or more. But eventually they all end the same way: with a miniature explosion that may fire off a small piece of the atom at incredible speed.

Each bit that flies off the exploding atom carries with it energy. Remember, this energy is just star energy, originally stored in the atom by the supernova explosion itself. But where does the energy go? Much of it turns into heat.

STAR POWER

The interior of the Earth is hot. We observe this heat in volcanoes, geysers, hot springs, and the deep-sea hydrothermal vents we met at the beginning of the chapter. Some of this heat can be traced to the energy of formation from our planet's ancient past. But were this the Earth's only source of heat, our planet's interior would have long ago grown cold. In fact, the heat still found deep inside the Earth is a lingering memory of those long-ago exploded stars. The radioactive atoms built in supernova explosions even now fuel the Earth's interior furnace, one tiny explosion at a time. We and the turtle live just above the still-simmering remains of ancient stellar explosions.

One consequence of this ancient energy is all the volcanic activity of our planet, the hot springs, the deep-sea vents, and the life they support. It is even possible that life first stirred within these pockets of warmth, heated from below by the remnants of ancient star power. We shall soon see that this gift of radioactive atoms from those faraway and long-dead stars is also the essential ingredient that makes our planet an ideal home for the sea turtle.

CHAPTER THREE

*T*he turtle is old. She has passed this way many times before. Unlike other animals that bluster and rush through life, the turtle moves slowly. She did not mate for the first time until her thirtieth year. Even now, she mates and lays eggs only once every two to four years of her life. She knows that she has time.

Turtles as a group are long-lived, too, though their origin is shrouded by the immensity of time. The first turtles must have appeared well over 220 million years ago, for it is from rocks of this age that we have extracted fossils of the most ancient turtle we know. Called Proganochelys, this was a very primitive creature (unlike living turtles, Proganochelys had teeth) and yet a very familiar one. In many ways, Proganochelys looked like a modern snapping turtle. Certainly there must be older turtle ancestors, buried *deeper in the rocks, but because we have yet to find them, the true origin of turtles remains a mystery.*

Though there are land-loving turtles, majestic island giants, and shade-loving desert dwellers, turtles as a group are mostly water creatures. Even as far back as 200 million years ago, some turtles had abandoned the freshwater of rivers and lakes and returned to the salty sea of their truly ancient ancestors. Though their names have changed, sea turtles today live much the same lives as those first sea turtles from so long ago. The sea turtle's way is both ancient and enduring.

TIME AND THE TURTLE

The Earth is about four and a half billion years old. Written out, that is 4,500,000,000 years. Scientists work with numbers like this one all the time, but what do such large numbers really mean? How can we possibly contemplate a number of years two million times longer than our entire written history?

Compared to any historical event, like the fall of Rome, for instance, the age of the Earth is immense. Even compared to the beginning of our own species perhaps a million years ago, four and a half billion years is overwhelming. But turtles are ancient creatures, having known the Earth for many millions of years before humans first appeared. Perhaps we can use turtles as our measuring stick to tame the age of the Earth.

WATER CLOCK

The oldest sea turtle we know lived around two hundred million years ago. Ever since then, there have been turtles swimming the seas of Earth. Suppose we represent the time of the sea turtle by a single glass (maybe sixteen ounces) of water. The glass is about three inches wide and five inches high. This glass of water, then, is our timeline, representing two hundred million years, over seventy billion of our days.

Working from the bottom up, we find that dinosaurs first appeared at just about the bottom of the glass, almost two hundred million years ago, then suddenly disappeared about sixty-five million years ago, a little over an inch and a half from the top. The last common ancestor of humans and chimpanzees appeared around six million years ago, about an eighth of an inch from the top of the glass. By comparison, all our written history (around three thousand years' worth) makes up much less than a single drop of water in the glass.

GLASSES OF TIME

Now that we have our measuring stick, let's work in the other direction. If that one glass of water represents the two hundred million years of sea turtles, how many glasses came before? The glass just before the turtle's glass takes us back to four hundred million years ago. Somewhere around the middle of that glass, perhaps around three hundred million years in the past, the first recognizable turtle must have appeared. Exactly where in the glass it would be, we still do not know.

At the bottom of this second glass, four hundred million years ago, we find the first fish. Among these fish was a creature (as yet unknown to us) whose descendants would, over millions of years, invade the land, evolve hard shells, and then carry those shells back to the sea. This creature is a common ancestor of both the turtle and ourselves. It would make a fascinating story itself, but we've only just begun our journey back in time. Let's keep moving.

The third glass takes us back to six hundred million years ago. This glass holds an event called the Cambrian Explosion, a time when the sea practically boiled with complex, intricate animals. There were no fish yet among these animals, but there was a tiny, wriggling, vaguely fishy creature whose descendants would one day both fill the seas and dominate the land. We will meet this creature again later in our

story. For now, we only wave hello as we continue our journey backward.

Glasses four and five take us back to one billion years ago. Around this time, the very first animals appeared, tiny ocean-borne creatures we would scarcely have noticed. Another five glasses takes us back to two billion years ago, a time when there were no animals, when all life on Earth consisted of single-celled bacteria. Already, these microbes had made enormous advances and had profoundly changed their world. In many important ways, it was the efforts of these tiny organisms that created the living world we know today. We will discover just how they did it later in our tale.

Thirteen more glasses take us beyond the very first living things on our planet, to a time when the Earth was battered and pummeled by a rain of space debris. Just above the bottom of this first glass, soon after the Earth itself formed, we witness an event that nearly tore our planet apart, but with a result both profound and beautiful. You call that result the Moon. We will soon learn more about the Moon's birth and discover just how important it is to the turtle and to us.

That's twenty-three glasses of water—a large number, but not an overwhelming one. The world seems old to us, because we are very young. To a sea turtle, whose turtle ancestors have swum the world's oceans for one twenty-third of our planet's history, the world isn't that old, after all.

CHAPTER FOUR

*T*he onion-white Moon pulls at the sea as the turtle approaches a long, thin strip of sand. She has been here before; sea turtles return to the same beach to build their nests again and again throughout their lives. It is likely that, decades before, our turtle herself hatched on a beach very near this one.

For several days, the turtle will swim offshore and mate. Many male turtles will vie for her attention. The successful males will provide her with sperm and then swim away to pursue yet another conquest. Our turtle collects sperm from many males, then stores the sperm within her body. The turtle's eggs, even those laid in the same nest, often have different fathers.

While female turtles return to their nesting beaches only once every two to four years, most male turtles mate more frequently, perhaps as often as every year of their adult lives.

Once a male turtle leaves the beach as a hatchling, he need never return to the land. Not so for our turtle. Tied to the land by her need to lay eggs, the female must choose both the right beach to ascend and the right time to climb it.

On some beaches with long slow slopes, the cycles of the Moon become vitally important to the turtle. She will wait until evening high tide to emerge, for the journey up the sand will be a difficult one. The deep water of the lunar high tide will carry the turtle closer to her final destination, a spot just above the very highest high tide line. She must lay her eggs above this line to keep them safe from a deadly soaking in seawater. Yet the eggs must not be too far from the waves, for the greater the distance her babies must crawl to reach water, the longer their odds of survival become.

SKY COMPASS

Look up at the sky and examine the Moon. Where is it in the sky? What time of night is it? Or is it even night-time at all? Some people are surprised to spot the Moon during the day. In fact, the location of the Moon in the sky at a particular time of the day or night follows a pattern that is just as regular and predictable as the far more familiar changing phases of our planet's satellite.

When the Moon is full, it is opposite the Sun in the sky, so that when the Sun is setting, the Moon is rising. When the Moon is nearly overhead in the afternoon, it is chasing the Sun toward the horizon. The side toward the Sun is the lit side, of course, and so the lit side of the Moon (the right side, if you're in the Northern Hemisphere) must face west. Just the opposite is true if you see the Moon high in the sky in the early morning. Its lit side (the Moon's left side, from the Northern Hemisphere) will face east, as the soon-to-rise Sun chases the Moon across the vault of the sky.

Our Moon is a strange and wonderful object. Its large size relative to its planet makes our satellite almost unique in the solar system, and maybe beyond. How did this amazing body come to be? The story of its origin, a story we humans have only recently learned, is an incredible tale of disaster and rebirth.

ENDINGS AND BEGINNINGS

Around four and a half billion years ago, the Earth was new, and no Moon circled our world. Then, one fateful day, a planet about the size of Mars crossed the Earth's path. Our young planet and this wanderer collided, an event that would have made an awesome spectacle had anyone been around to witness it. The collision nearly destroyed the Earth, but it did destroy the other world. That world was pulverized, and its shattered remnants, along with a large chunk of our planet, were blasted into space. Much of the debris formed a ring around the Earth, a bit like the ring that today encircles the planet Saturn.

The Earth's ring condensed slowly into a single large

ball that became the Moon. In the beginning, the Moon was much closer to Earth than we find it today. It would have appeared enormous. It was so near it caused huge tides that would have flooded any continents many miles inland. Slowly, as the friction from these great tides reduced our planet's rate of spin, the Moon itself spiraled away, growing ever farther and, as seen from Earth, ever smaller in the sky.

Even now, our two worlds are engaged in an elegant

dance, as the Moon spirals ever so slowly away from the Earth, and in response the Earth's rotation slows. The change is tiny, but real. If the Earth and Moon were to survive long enough, in something over a trillion years the Earth's rate of spin would match the Moon's speed through the sky. The Moon would then not move as seen from our planet, but would instead hang motionless in our skies for all eternity.

THE TURTLE AND THE MOON

We can be grateful for our strange, unlikely companion, despite the violent past it reveals. Only one other body in our solar system, tiny frozen Pluto with its icy moon Charon, comes anywhere near the Earth and Moon in relative world-to-satellite size. The Moon is huge compared to Mars's two diminutive satellites. Mercury and Venus lack moons altogether, and the giant planets beyond Mars dwarf even their largest moons by huge margins.

The presence of such a relatively large and nearby Moon makes a profound difference for life on our world. The Moon and Sun drive our tides. Without the Moon, these tides would be smaller and of less consequence. The daily rhythm of the tides affects the lives of many species. As we've seen, sea turtles that nest on shallow sloping beaches time their nesting with the tides, crawling up the beach at high tide, both to conserve energy and to swim over otherwise impassable objects such as coral reefs.

Even more important, the Moon keeps stable the tilt of the Earth's axis. It is our planet's tilt that is responsible for the seasons. Many delicate ecosystems depend on the regularity of the seasons—the cooling of summer heat in the longer nights of fall, the thawing of winter snow in the warm days of spring. Without the Moon, our planet's axis might shift over time, with disastrous results for many living things. Over millions of years, polar regions could drift into equatorial warmth; rain forests might slide into the frigid darkness of the poles. Sea turtles would not be alone in suffering great harm from such changes.

Without the Moon we would be living (or not living) on a very different world. And yet the Moon's existence is an accident, the result of an unlikely collision in our solar system's earliest days. It's really an amazing thought. Up there, orbiting far above us, is a piece of the ancient Earth, blasted away from us four and a half billion years ago. Much of the world we know today simply could not be without the beautiful remains of that ancient catastrophe.

CHAPTER FIVE

The first people of North America called their home Turtle Island. This is the story they told.

At first, there was no land. Water covered the world, and the people lived among the clouds. One day, the daughter of the chief of the cloud people found a tree growing in the clouds. The girl pulled the tree up by its roots, and through the hole in the clouds she saw water far below. Losing her balance, the girl fell through the hole, pulling the tree behind her as she went.

The girl plunged toward the water and landed with a splash. She would have drowned, if not for the turtle. Seeing the girl struggle in the water, the turtle floated to the surface. The other animals gathered nearby and helped the girl onto the turtle's back. Then the turtle said to the animals, "Swim to the bottom of the sea and there gather mud from the roots of the tree that fell from the sky. Bring the mud and spread it on my back."

One by one, the animals swam down to the mud. But the sea was vast and deep, and some of the animals drowned before they could return. Finally, tiny muskrat emerged with a ball of mud in her mouth. The animals spread the mud on the turtle's shell, and the shell began to grow. The mud buckled and cracked, becoming mountains and river valleys, and the turtle's shell became the land. The girl called to her people in the clouds, showing them that the land was good. The people came down from their home in the clouds and built their world on the back of the turtle. And even today, the people still live on this land and call it Turtle Island.

SINKING STONES

Pick up a stone and toss it into the water. It sinks like, well, like a stone. This is an ordinary event, yet it reveals a great puzzle. If a stone sinks in water, then how did it come to be above water in the first place? Why is there dry land at all?

Imagine the Earth with all its water removed. Glancing at this dried-out Earth, you would see lowlands (the ocean basins) and uplands (the continents). The difference in their heights is surprisingly small—the Pacific Ocean, for instance, is around eight thousand miles wide in many places but averages only about two and a half miles deep. Its deepest point, the Marianas Trench off the coast of Guam, is only seven miles below the surface. Were you to reduce the entire Pacific Ocean to the size of a football field, the ocean basins would average about one inch deep, barely enough water to get your shoes wet. The ocean is much, much wider than it is deep.

Build a model of North America alongside your Pacific Ocean model and you'd find that the height of the land is even less impressive than the depth of the ocean. On the same scale as the Pacific-become-football-field, North America would have an average height of about a quarter of an inch, and its highest peaks would be around an inch and a half up. Clearly, there is more than enough space within the ocean basins to hold all the land, were someone to toss it, stone by stone, into the sea. (Of course, were this to happen the water level itself would rise ever higher, covering much of the land even before it was all thrown into the sea.)

But this is just the experiment that has been happening on our planet for billions of years. Running water—rainwater, meltwater from icy glaciers, the running water of creeks, streams, and rivers—and moving air have been and are even now eroding the land, breaking it down and carrying it bit by bit into the sea. So why hasn't the Earth been worn smooth? Why, instead of a planetwide ocean, is there dry land at all?

The first Americans answered that question with a tale about the turtle, an animal they knew well. But science has found another answer, even more profound and far-reaching. The answer is found not on the back of the turtle, but rather far below the deepest ocean trench, in a place where the rocks flow like molasses.

THE BIG APPLE

The Earth is built a little like an apple. The apple's thin skin represents a layer of Earth called the crust. The crust holds all the oceans, all the land, all the mountains, valleys, and turtle-nesting beaches of our planet. Below this thin crust is a layer of hot, flowing rock called the mantle (represented by the flesh of the apple). Finally, deep below the mantle is the even hotter molten and solid core of the Earth, in proportion close to the size of the apple's core.

Though our day-to-day lives are dominated by events here on the crust of the Earth, movements within the mantle can have a profound effect on the land and the water far above. Unlike the interior of an apple, the interior of our planet is hot. That heat moves from the inside to the outside, something like the movement of water in a heated pan.

In a pan, water moves from low (where the heat is) to high (where the water can release its heat) in a cir-

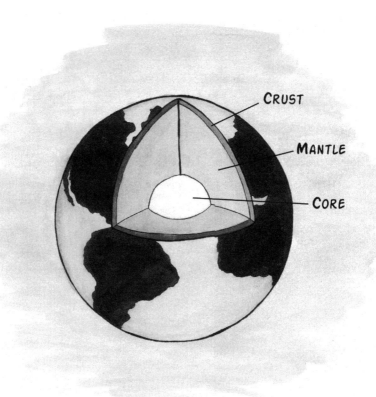

cular motion called a convection current. Air can move in the same way, heating up near the ground, then cooling as it rises. The rock of the mantle is solid but so hot and under so much pressure that it moves in a convection current as well, though compared to air or water this movement is very slow. Any spot within the mantle might take as long as ten thousand years to move from low to high, but of course ten thousand years is an eye blink for a four-and-a-half-billion-year-old planet.

THE SKIN OF THE EARTH

An apple's skin is attached to its flesh, but the crust of the Earth is not so firmly attached to the mantle. Instead, driven by heat welling up from below, the crust can move and shift across the Earth's surface. This movement, slow, steady, and unstoppable, is called plate tectonics, and is the most important source of dry land on our planet today.

The Earth's crust is broken into plates. Like chunks of ice on a frozen lake, the plates are separated by cracks and fissures called faults. These cracks mark the boundaries of the plates covering the surface of the Earth, from mountaintop to ocean floor.

Crust comes in two varieties. Ocean crust is denser, while the crust of the continents is less dense. Just as helium balloons float in air, continental crust stubbornly floats above the level of the ocean crust, even when two plates collide. And it is the collision of plates that drives the land toward the sky.

MOUNTAINS FROM WITHIN

If two sections of continental crust collide, the land on the plates can crumple like a car hood in a traffic accident. The result is a mountain chain—the Himalayas in Asia are the most famous example, the product of a collision between Asia and India.

If a collision brings together ocean and continental crust, the denser ocean crust slides under the lighter continental crust. The ocean crust, melting in the hot, dense mantle below, rises upward and boosts the land above, causing great mountains to rise. The mountains and volcanoes on the western side of North and South America formed in this way, when ocean crust of the Pacific plate slid under continental crust of the North American and South American plates. In some places, molten rock has even poked through the surface, resulting in volcanoes.

Our planet is an active world. Wind and water erode the land, carrying sediments into the sea. Far below, the heat of the Earth drives the movement of the plates, pushes them into one another, and shoves mountains skyward despite the eroding power of water and wind. It is just this constant growth of mountains that keeps at least a little of our planet beyond the reach of the sea, high enough and dry enough for us and the turtle.

HEAT FROM THE STARS

The question of why the Earth is hot inside remained a profound puzzle until the discovery of radioactivity just over one hundred years ago. It was found then that some minerals, those laced with radioactive atoms such as uranium and thorium, pour heat energy into their rocky neighbors deep within the Earth. They do this by exploding, one tiny atom at a time, over billions of years. As we saw in chapter 2, the ultimate source of that energy, the creators of those unstable atoms that will one day burst apart and release their pent-up energy to the rocks, are giant exploding stars.

This is an amazing trail to follow, and we can see it now in its full glory. Billions of years ago, a giant star died in a supernova explosion. Some of the energy from that explosion went into building new atoms, and some of those atoms were unstable. Swept up by the new planet Earth, those unstable atoms rested deep within. For any one atom, billions of years might have passed quietly. But the day came finally when this energy stored so long ago was released. The atom exploded, firing off a miniature bullet that warmed the nearby rocks by a miniscule amount. Atom by atom, day after day, year after year, those tiny explosions added their energy to the heat of the Earth. They are doing so even now, every moment of every day. And the Earth moves. The sliding plates press into one another, and the crust buckles, warps, sinks, and rises. The pushed-up land lies just out of reach of the salty sea, allowing in time the formation of high desert plains, lush rainforests, and long, thin strips of sand where a sea turtle may return again to lay her eggs by starlight.

CHAPTER SIX

*T*he turtle emerges in silence. She watches for any disturbance. If something is not to her liking, she will return to the sea, emerging further on to resume her work or even waiting a day or more to try again. Eventually, though, the turtle will complete this final leg of her journey, the most dangerous hours she has faced since her own frantic first days of life.

Slowly, the turtle works her way up the sandy beach. The flippers that function so well in water are clumsy on land, and her heavy shell is unwieldy. Salt glands near her eyes form tears on the turtle's cheeks as she crawls. She is not crying, but instead removing sea salt from her body. Her tears may serve a second function on land, clearing the turtle's eyes of the sand she will soon fling wildly as she begins the difficult task of building her egg chamber.

The turtle digs the chamber with her hind limbs. She alternates left and right, scooping up sand and carrying it

out on delicately curved flippers. Mounds of sand build slowly around her until she flings it away to make room for more. She digs until her flippers can no longer reach the chamber bottom. Then the eggs come.

Most sea turtles lay around a hundred Ping-Pong-ballsized eggs. They are not rigid like chicken eggs, but some-

what rubbery and flexible. This is fortunate, as the first of the eggs face a precipitous fall into a deep pit and the others must land on top of the early arrivals.

When all her eggs have been laid, the turtle carefully covers her work, hiding the signs of her labor. She trudges toward the sea, a journey made longer now because the tide has likely receded. She stops often to rest, exhausted by her efforts. As she reaches the surf, the waves wash the sand from her face, flippers, and back. The incoming water buoys her heavy body, and finally she is gone, disappearing into the waves as silently as she came.

MOUNTAINS TO THE SEA

Stand on a beach and look out at the ocean. You are poised at the edge of two worlds, the two worlds the sea turtle has inherited from her ancient lineage. She is utterly at home in the ocean water, yet she depends on this thin strip of sand for the most important activity of her life. Without the building of nests and the laying of eggs in this warm sand, the sea turtle would have vanished long ago. It may surprise you to learn that the beach sand where this drama unfolds came not from the ocean water before you, but rather from the land at your back.

Each sand grain tells a story. The story of many sand grains starts high on a mountaintop, where a drop of

rain splashes on a smooth, weather-worn rock. The raindrop combines with millions more to form a fast-flowing mountain stream. Bit by bit, this stream will carry its mountain down, down to the sea.

Sand is not all the same kind of material, like strawberries, diamonds, or turtle eggs. Instead of being defined by its composition, sand is defined by its size. Grains bigger than sand are called gravel. Grains smaller are called silt or clay. Everything in between, whether white, black, tan, or auburn, is sand.

Unlike materials such as sugar or salt, sand does not dissolve in water. But it can be moved by water if the water flows swiftly enough. The faster the water flows, the larger the bits of stuff it can push along. High on a mountain, where the streambed is steep, the water moves quickly and may push sand or gravel along with it. Even boulders may roll along the streambed in the swiftest of streams. Further down the mountain, the streambed flattens and slows, and the boulders, gravel, and sand come to rest. A sand grain might rest in one place, more or less, for millions of years, but then, as the streambed changes, the water rushes through, and the sand may move once again. Bit by bit, the landscape is altered.

The change might be a hundred years' flood, when the water pours down from the mountains and spills from its banks. Or the change might signal the end of an ice age, as glaciers melt and water flows seaward in uncontrolled torrents. Nothing on our planet is forever; change will come in time. Step by step, the sand grain approaches the sea.

RECYCLED GRAINS

Some sand grains are made of many bits and pieces of rock, cemented together, ripped apart, then cemented again. It's hard to imagine these tiny grains with such a violent history, but under a microscope a sand grain's traumatic past becomes more clear. Edges are scraped, corners are torn or broken off, and pieces are haphazardly connected to form a jumbled mass of minerals. Oddly, wind can often do more damage than water—the collision of wind-blown sand grains can be surprisingly damaging. Grains that have spent most of their time in water, by contrast, show signs of a less stressful past.

If you scoop up a handful of sand at the seashore, you will see that it is a mixture of many different things. Mostly sand is rock, remains of mountains, sea cliffs, and boulders that were. Some bits of sand may be first-generation grains, newly formed from fresh volcanic rock. Others may be the washed-out remnants of a type of rock called sandstone. Sandstone is just sand, cemented together by time and pressure into solid rock. If the grain came from sandstone, it might be very old, indeed, for it likely existed as sand long before the sandstone itself was formed. Some of these grains may be many millions of years old, having witnessed many times over the cycles of the sea turtle: the laying of eggs, the struggle to reach the sea, the return of the next generation many years later. What stories the sand might tell.

STAR CHILDREN

The most common sand on turtle-nesting beaches is made from a mineral called quartz. Quartz is built of two elements, silicon and oxygen. We've already witnessed the birth of these elements within a hot, dying star. Both owe their existence to carbon, that element formed through the unlikely combination of fast-moving helium and unstable beryllium. We've seen how carbon then fuses with helium and even with itself to create a variety of more complex atoms, including both oxygen and silicon. Without this path through carbon, none of the more complex elements could be. Sand, like the sea turtle, is a child of carbon.

It's a wondrous tale. The turtle, a machine made of carbon, buries her own children, pieces of herself encased in shell, in a chamber built from sand. But the sand itself is built from elements forged long ago amid the collisions of carbon atoms in the super-hot depths of a dying star. To build a turtle, or a sandy beach, you must first create a universe that is good at making carbon.

CHAPTER SEVEN

*S*urrounded by their blanket of sand, the baby turtles undergo a transformation no less miraculous than the development of human babies within the womb. While a human child has an ever-present mother who can supply food and water, remove waste, maintain a proper temperature, and otherwise protect her unborn baby, a sea turtle egg enjoys no such protection. What a staggering change, from a loose collection of liquids within a soft white shell to an active and eager young turtle in only two months. How does this transformation happen? The answers are energy and information.

The energy comes almost entirely from the mother turtle, offered up willingly as the egg is formed. Each egg contains all the food and nearly all the water required to build a baby turtle. The eggshell itself is permeable, allowing gases and water to enter. But the majority of the *raw materials required to make a baby turtle must reside within the egg from the beginning.*

It is just this stored energy that makes the turtle egg such an inviting target for thieves. The list of creatures that actively seek out turtle eggs is a long one, and includes human beings. Other dangers come from storms like hurricanes, which might drown or uncover the eggs. Extreme dry weather can kill the eggs, too. Most turtle mothers build three to seven nests in a season, in the hopes that at least one will develop undisturbed.

Energy alone, however, is not enough. The egg must also contain information. This comes, in equal parts, from the father and the mother. Deep within each of the baby turtle's rapidly dividing cells, in a central nodule called the nucleus, is a spaghetti-like tangle of long, thin molecules called DNA. Each collection of DNA is literally a recipe for building a new turtle. The recipe is pasted together—half from the mother, half from the father—to create a unique turtle within every egg. There are so many possible combinations of turtle DNA that no two turtles are ever exactly alike. Each new baby is a celebration of what can be.

A FAST START

One of the most profound discoveries of science is that all life comes from a single common ancestor. It didn't have to be that way. We might have found unique, unrelated ancestors for plants and animals, or certain kinds of strange bacteria. Instead, no matter where we look on this planet, we find that all life is of a single kind. Every living thing on our planet shares a common heritage. The story of life is an unbroken chain, stretching from the shadowy past of four billion years ago to now, the very moment you read these words.

Life appeared on our planet almost as soon as it could. The young Earth was glowing hot and punished by a rain of ice, rock, and metal from space. Asteroids, meteorites, and comets blasted the Earth, converting their great speed into yet more heat on the blistering young planet. One of those collisions, as we have seen, gave rise to our Moon.

As the deluge from space finally slowed, a new deluge, this one of liquid water, cooled and healed the surface. Rivers, lakes, and oceans formed, and a lovely blue planet slowly emerged from the bruised and pock-marked world that was.

Within this blanket of water, somehow, a new thing formed: life. The details are mysterious. Some scientists believe that life first formed at the bottom of the new oceans, at the hot hydrothermal vents we met in chapter 2. Others think life might have begun on water-covered beds of clay. Some even suggest that life, either fully formed or else well on its way, could have arrived from space on a comet or a meteorite.

However it began, one thing is clear: life is built

from the stuff of the universe. The ingredients of life—carbon, oxygen, hydrogen, and the other elements that make up turtles and all other living things—are no different from those that make up the air, the seas, the rocks and sands of Earth. But these elements are not unique to our planet. As we have seen, they are found, and formed, in the stars. Life emerges from this universe; it is a part of the universe.

That all life on Earth shares a common ancestor becomes clear when we look at the details of living things. Somewhere near the beginning, probably well more than three billion years ago, life on Earth hit on a particular collection of atoms, a molecule called DNA, to serve as its recipe book. The language with which the book is written and read is common to all living things. We each contain this same book inside us today, with minor variations that make us what we are: turtles, bacteria, oak trees, and humans.

THE AGE OF BACTERIA

For the first three billion years or so, bacteria were the most complex life-forms on Earth. This is no insult, as bacteria are marvelously complex. Bacteria solved all the major problems of life early on. Critically, they found ways to make their own food from sunlight. In the process they released oxygen, a dangerous waste gas for the bacteria but an indispensable food-burning chemical for sea turtles and all other animals.

Bacteria solved lots of other problems as well. They found ways to move through their watery world. They found ways to combat disease. They found ways to kill. They even found ways to trade their DNA with one another, in this way gaining new survival tools from other successful strains. Then, around a billion years ago, bacteria began actively working together.

TOGETHERNESS

Bacteria are amazing living machines, capable of chemical and biological feats far beyond our most advanced engineering. But bacteria are not turtles. Besides the obvious differences, a big difference can be found in the structures of living cells. Bacterial cells are called prokaryotes. They do not contain a central nucleus to house their DNA. They are also mostly missing the specialized cellular structures called organelles.

By contrast, sea turtles (and all other animals, including ourselves) are eukaryotes. Within a turtle cell, DNA is tucked safely away in the cell nucleus.* Just outside the nucleus, the real business of turtle life takes place. Organelles called mitochondria receive fuel

---

*The cell nucleus is not to be confused with the atomic nucleus we met in chapter 1. While the cell's nucleus is very small on the scale of a human or a sea turtle, it is much larger than an atomic nucleus, and in fact is made up of tens of trillions of atoms.

from the turtle's blood and transform it into usable energy. Other organelles direct the construction of proteins, the building blocks of the turtle's body. Most of the work of being a turtle is, in fact, performed by the organelles found inside her every cell.

To discover the origin of nearly all these organelles, we travel back a billion years or more to witness a series of events that would change life on Earth forever. In some long-forgotten sea or shallow pool, two bacteria come together. Perhaps the larger bacterium tries to eat the smaller one, or the smaller tries to infect the larger. Instead of destroying each other, though, the two microbes find that life together is better than life apart. The smaller bacterium becomes the organelle, the larger a new kind of cell, called a eukaryote. Many scientists today think that many, even most, of the important structures in eukaryotic cells—including even the nucleus that holds our DNA—first arose in a process something like this. Each of our cells, then, might be an alliance of former adversaries, living in peace now for billions of years.

In time, eukaryotic cells themselves would learn to work together, and this would lead to the evolution of large, multicelled creatures such as animals and plants. An enormous array of these new living things evolved, filling the Earth's oceans with never-before-seen diversity and complexity. And some of those eukaryotes lead us to the turtle.

TIME AND CHANGE

Between five and six hundred million years ago, a small and unassuming creature evolved a nerve cord. One of its descendants, among the first animals we know with such a feature, was a flattened two-inch-long wormlike swimmer known as *Pikaia gracelens*.

Evolution is a risky proposition. Most of the animals that have evolved on Earth have vanished without a trace. Some, such as the buglike trilobites, swarmed in the oceans and seas for hundreds of millions of years, before, during, and after the time of *Pikaia*. Yet despite their fantastic success, there are no living trilobites anywhere on Earth today. Their closest surviving relatives are a group of animals that includes spiders.

Pikaia lived among creatures that were bigger, faster, and more dangerous than itself. Yet against the odds, *Pikaia* and its body plan survived. In time, the nerve cord of *Pikaia* evolved into the spinal cord found in all vertebrates, from fish to amphibians to you, me, and the sea turtle. *Pikaia's* legacy lives on.

How could all these changes take place? After all, bacteria produce more bacteria, and turtles more turtles. We never see a turtle egg produce a frog instead. How does evolution happen at all? The DNA molecule holds the answer. DNA is copied, like some precious ancient document, from generation to generation in all living things. But if these copies were never any different from the originals, then indeed evolution would grind to a halt. Instead, rarely, changes called mutations appear. Even more rarely, a mutation proves beneficial. One surprising source of mutations takes us back to the stars.

STAR BULLETS

We've already learned that stars explode and that in these stellar catastrophes huge amounts of energy are released. Some of that energy takes the form of a burst of particles, high-speed atomic nuclei hurled at unbelievable speeds into deep space. We call these particles cosmic rays.

Cosmic rays are ideal space bullets. If these bullets reach the Earth, they don't travel very far before they smash into obstacles—usually atoms in our air. A spray of new particles erupts from the impact site. These new particles might also collide with atoms in the air, setting off yet more particle showers, and so on until whatever is left reaches our planet's surface.

Thousands of these particles pass through your body every day. Thousands more pass through turtle eggs as they develop within their blanket of sand. Suppose one of these bullets smashes into a strand of turtle DNA. The collision may change the text of the DNA molecule, the way a fallen drop of water may blur a word in an ancient manuscript. If left undisturbed by the cell's proofreading mechanisms, this collision site becomes a mutation, a change that is permanently stored in the DNA of the turtle's cell. Most mutations are harmless. Some mutations can kill the cell. If the cell happens to be one of just a few in a developing turtle embryo, the mutation can kill the turtle, too. But very rarely a mutation might help the turtle embryo—maybe making it a little better at digesting food, a little better at fighting disease, or perhaps even a little smarter.

This is still a long way from changing a turtle into another creature altogether. It is worth remembering that turtles have been around for hundreds of millions of years with relatively few changes. The turtle's way of life has been successful for a long time, and it is difficult for a mutation to improve upon it. On the other hand, mammals have evolved from a group of shrew-like insect eaters into whales, elephants, jaguars, orangutans, and us, to name just a few, in an evolutionary spurt began in earnest only sixty-five million years ago. Not coincidentally this spurt began just as the dinosaurs that had dominated life on land finally disappeared, opening a new world for our mammal ancestors. Evolution requires both time and opportunity.

Not all mutations are caused by cosmic ray collisions. Others are due to the natural radioactivity of the Earth. As we've seen, that radioactivity is another product of long-ago exploded stars. Still other mutations can be traced to the DNA-copying machinery of the cell. Some mutations have causes we still don't understand. But at least some of the story of evolution, we can now see, was and is written by cosmic rays; bullets from deep space, shot by chance through DNA molecules. In yet another way, we and the turtle owe our existence to the stars.

CHAPTER EIGHT

*N*ear the middle of their time in the nest, a change comes to the baby turtles. It is a change that will profoundly affect their adult lives. Beneath their blanket of sand, the turtles gradually become either female or male. Surprisingly, the change is triggered by the temperature of the sand itself.

Humans and other mammals become male or female at the moment of conception. Our gender is determined by the portion of our DNA delivered by our fathers. Birds employ a similar strategy, though their gender is determined by DNA from their mothers. But sea turtles are different. Every sea turtle baby possesses within its own DNA the recipe for building both male and female turtles. The turtle's future fate is determined by which set of instructions gets switched on.

We do not yet know just how one set of instructions is

switched on and the other switched off. But we do know that temperature controls this critical change. Sometimes the temperature within a nest falls into just the right range to allow a mixture of male and female turtles. More often, sea turtles from the same nest will be either all female or all male. High temperatures create females, future mothers that may one day return to build their own nests of sand. Low temperatures make males, destined (if they survive their first frantic moments on the beach) to disappear into the waves, never to appear on land again as long as they live.

GIRL OR BOY?

The turtle's method of becoming male or female may seem strange to us. In fact, many animals have even stranger methods of determining a gender. Some animals possess both male and female sex organs; these animals are called hermaphrodites and include the ordinary earthworm. Other animals, including some snails, change gender during their lifetimes, while still others become one gender or the other only after being infected by a particular bacterium.

The sea turtle's habit of fixing its gender by temperature could be just an evolutionary leftover from an earlier ancestor. But it is also possible that this temperature-dependent gender selection is an adaptation to the environment. It may be that in warmer climates there are benefits to producing female hatchlings, while in colder climates the benefit may work the other way. One potential problem with temperature-dependent sex is that the environment is not constant. Sea turtles have swum the world's oceans for at least two hundred million years, and in that time the Earth's climate has swung between extremes: from a global hothouse to a worldwide ice age. Wouldn't such changes disrupt the turtle's delicately balanced system? Wouldn't a too-cold world, for instance, produce all male sea turtles, leaving no one to lay the eggs?

It is important to remember that our view of sea turtles is very much limited to our own time. Except for a few fossils (which don't tell us much about how ancient turtles reproduced), all we know about sea turtles comes from living species. But these species are not constant. They are ever-changing. In fact, every turtle is slightly different from every other turtle, even within the same species. These differences are small, but over many generations these variations cause turtle populations to change, to drift, to adapt to altered conditions. There are differences right now, for instance, in the temperature that determines gender among living turtle populations, depending on where those sea turtles usually nest. Evolution never stops, and sea turtle populations have been evolving for their entire two-hundred-million-year history. They are evolving now and will continue to evolve as long as they exist.

There is, however, one certain way to prevent a group of organisms from evolving. That way is to drive the group to extinction. And this may be just what we are doing to the sea turtle.

UNLEASHING THE SUN

While there are many dangers to sea turtles and their land- and freshwater-dwelling cousins all over the world, one of the trickiest of these dangers may be human-caused global warming. To see how humans might be altering the Earth's climate, recall the role played by carbon in all living things. Trees are made mostly of carbon and oxygen, but where do they get it? The surprising answer is this: a tree is built chiefly from air.

As they grow, trees pull carbon and oxygen from the air, in the form of a gas called carbon dioxide. They use the energy of the Sun to chemically combine carbon dioxide with hydrogen from water to make the energy-rich sugars and other building blocks that go into making a tree. You can think of a tree as a collection of air, water, and sunlight, all tied together with chemistry.

Under ordinary conditions, when a tree dies these ingredients are broken apart and returned to the environment. The energy of all that sunlight is released as the tree is consumed by animals, bacteria, and fungi. Water reenters the ground and the atmosphere, and carbon dioxide returns to the air.

If conditions are a little different, however, trees might not decay in the normal way. During a time on Earth called the Carboniferous Period, trees died and fell into acidic swamps where normal decay couldn't take place. Instead, over many thousands of years, trees

were squeezed together and slowly transformed into energy-rich coal. A similar series of events turned ocean organisms into oil, as the carbon and carbon-rich compounds stored during life became squeezed and concentrated in death. When we burn these concentrated substances in our furnaces, car engines, and power plants, the energy we're releasing is just sunlight, built up over thousands of years and then unleashed in the course of an afternoon.

This stored-up sunlight drives our technology. But as the energy from coal and oil powers our world, the carbon on which it rides is released into the air, becoming (once again) carbon dioxide gas. There's nothing unnatural about this gas. Without at least a little carbon dioxide in the air, plants couldn't grow at all. All animals on Earth, from worms to sea turtles to humans, release carbon dioxide every day as a normal part of living. But our rapid burning of coal and oil is releasing millions of years' worth of carbon dioxide into the atmosphere in a geologic eye blink. The normal pathways for removing this carbon dioxide from the air are overwhelmed. Excess carbon dioxide is building in the atmosphere, and that affects the climate.

Most scientists today are convinced that global temperatures have risen in recent decades and that a major cause of the temperature rise is the extra carbon dioxide gas we've pumped into the air. Carbon dioxide affects the way the Earth radiates heat into space, and that drives up temperatures. With higher temperatures, more ocean water evaporates, and this extra water vapor drives the temperature up even further. The climate is a complex system, and we are far from understanding all the consequences of even a small change in global temperatures. Whatever the larger effects, though, there is little doubt that even a small change in average temperature could have a big effect on the world's sea turtles.

HOT SAND, WET SAND

While sea turtles may be able to adapt to climate changes that happen over thousands or tens of thousands of years, the changes we're making in just hundreds or even tens of years may be too much for the turtle's slow, deliberate way of life. Recall how turtle eggs are affected by temperature. High temperatures produce female turtles, low temperatures males. If most of the world's turtle-nesting beaches become too hot to produce males, then perhaps eventually there will be few male turtles left.

A greater threat than gender imbalance may be the loss of nesting beaches altogether. As seawater warms, it takes up more space and begins to crawl up the beach. Just a small rise in ocean temperature could cause ocean water to drown coastlines, threatening human structures on those coasts. To protect our own creations, we might build seawalls to keep the water out. But such seawalls would keep out more than water. They would keep out the turtles as well.

Already weakened by our fishing nets, our pollution, and our love of turtle eggs and beachfront property, global warming could be the final push that drives sea turtles to extinction. Sea turtles may adapt to these changes, perhaps by moving to other, less developed, cooler nesting grounds. But these are already rare, and becoming scarcer. Perhaps sea turtles will have the time and the flexibility to adapt, or perhaps they will not. We simply don't yet know.

As nesting populations disappear, genetic diversity is lost. The lower the diversity in a population, the more vulnerable it becomes to other challenges, including disease and accidental death. These weakened sea turtle populations might continue to slide, until there are simply no turtles left.

There will be no fanfare, no final struggle for survival. The turtles will simply be gone. Extinction is permanent; once an animal is extinct, it is gone forever. It would be an unfortunate end to a group of creatures with such a long and distinguished history. Yet it is often true that life finds a way.

CHAPTER NINE

*D*eep within its covering of sand, the small round egg shudders. A jagged projection (the egg tooth) pushes through the shell, and a moment later a baby turtle emerges. All around her, the turtle's nest mates struggle to free themselves from their own eggs. The turtles climb, actually helping each other with their movements. Sand falling from above helps build a platform for the turtles below, while movement from below helps propel the turtles above.

As a group, the turtles pause just below the surface. If the temperature of the sand above them is too high, they cease their movements and wait. High temperature often means daylight, and a daylight emergence would bring almost certain death.

As night descends on the beach (or sometimes, as falling rain eases the heat of the day), the turtles erupt from the *sand. Instantly and almost without fail the hatchlings head straight for the sea. Their cue is the horizon glow over the ocean, reflected moonshine and starlight off the mirrorlike surface of the water. Having never touched the ocean nor seen the sky, the turtles scramble toward this gently beckoning light and away from the darker background of the land (unless a carelessly placed streetlight or porch lamp leads them astray).*

The hatchlings show a single-minded determination. If obstacles block their path, they climb over if they can, go around if they must. Some hatchlings will end their brief journey short of the water, captured by gulls, raccoons, armadillos, crabs, and domestic cats and dogs. For those turtles that reach the sea, a deadly gauntlet of predatory fish awaits. Yet somehow enough hatchlings escape this trial to carry turtle DNA through the generations. Perhaps one baby turtle in a thousand will survive.

Once they elude the dangers of the coast, most hatchlings head for the open ocean, an ocean they have never tasted, never touched, never seen. They will spend several years or even decades here. Some species hunt for tiny crabs and shrimp amid floating islands of seaweed found far from shore. Others drift in the currents of the open ocean, tiny specks of life surrounded by blue emptiness.

When they are large enough they will leave this home for the feeding grounds of their own species. Finally, twenty years or more since the day they hatched, the turtles will begin the long journey to the nesting beaches where they were born. For millions of years sea turtles have repeated this cycle, forming an unbroken chain through the generations. How much longer will this cycle continue? Only time can know.

TURTLES ALL THE WAY DOWN

There is an oft-repeated story about an astronomer lecturing on the origin, fate, and structure of the universe. He provides the current scientific view (the view you will read shortly in this final chapter), then invites questions. A lady in the crowd stands and says, "This is very nice what you've told us, but it is all wrong. The world is built on the backs of four elephants, and the elephants stand on the shell of a turtle."

The astronomer considers the lady and decides to ask a question himself. "If this is true," he says, "then what is the turtle standing on?"

"Oh, you are very clever," the lady replies, "but you can't fool me. It's turtles all the way down."

The lady's statement brings us face to face with the puzzles of extent and duration. Is the universe infinitely big? Is it eternal? Did it have a beginning and, perhaps more important, will it ever end?

THE SUN AND THE EARTH

We know a great deal about how the Sun and the Earth will end. Like other stars of its size, the Sun will one day, about five billion years from now, face a crisis when its hydrogen fuel runs low. The central part of the Sun will shrink and heat while the outer portion will swell into a cool, wispy red giant star.

Long before this happens, however, the aging Sun will have sterilized the Earth. Ever since the Sun formed, it has been slowly getting brighter. A brighter Sun means a hotter Earth. The change is very slow—much slower, for instance, than the change caused by excess carbon dioxide described in the previous chapter. About a billion years from now, the brighter Sun will heat the Earth until our oceans boil away into space. Little is likely to survive this change, and clearly sea turtles cannot live in a world with no seas.

But a billion years is a very long time. Perhaps our existence will make the difference. Perhaps sea turtles will swim in the belly of some interstellar marine park, built and operated by our own distant descendants. Perhaps we will store turtle DNA and grow our own sea turtle clones to crawl upon faraway ocean beaches. We can imagine a future in which Earthly life might somehow survive the Earth's demise. But what of the universe itself? What future does it face?

THE END AND THE BEGINNING

We've always wondered about the fate of the universe. Scientists, philosophers, and storytellers have thought and speculated. Only very recently, though, have scientists found new clues that may at last answer the question: Where is the universe going? Strangely, to understand the future of the universe we must travel into its past.

Space, it turns out, is getting bigger. About fourteen billion years ago (or roughly three times the age of the Earth), our universe began as a hot, dense fireball. As the fireball spread, it cooled and gave rise to atoms, stars, and galaxies. Most of those first atoms were hydrogen, the simplest atom. About a quarter were helium, the next-simplest atom. A tiny fraction were the third-simplest atom, lithium. All the other atoms that make up the universe today had to wait, as we have seen, to form inside the stars.

The explosion that began our universe is with us still. All the galaxies that we can see through our telescopes rush away from each other, and from us. In fact, it is not so much the galaxies but the so-called fabric of space, the universe itself, that is expanding. The galaxies are just along for the ride. How long will this expansion continue?

For many years, scientists speculated that the expansion of the universe might be slowing down. Such a slowing universe might stop expanding one day and begin to shrink, just as a rock thrown upward slows and then falls. The contraction might continue, it was thought, until all the galaxies crash back together in a "big crunch." Such an event would end our universe, erasing all that had existed before.

Yet recent measurements by several teams of scientists show that the universe is not slowing at all, but is instead expanding faster and faster as time passes. This is such a new and surprising discovery that scientists are still trying to determine what might be causing this universal speed-up. Whatever its cause, though, the acceleration of our universe likely means that we won't end in a "big crunch."

You might think this never-ending expansion gives our universe a cheery sort of immortality. But there's a problem. As we've seen, stars don't last forever. New stars are born, but eventually that process will stop, too. If the universe is around long enough, either all the hydrogen will be used up or else what is left will be spread so thin that no new stars can arise. As the old stars blink out, one by one, there eventually will be nothing to replace them. If there is no way to regenerate the universe, it is headed for a very long, very cold, very dark end.

OTHER WORLDS

Yet there is still so much we don't know. Most of all, we don't know why our universe is here, or even if such a question can have an answer. As many scientists have put it, "Why is there something rather than nothing?" What was the fireball that began our universe? What, if anything, caused it? What came "before" the fireball, or was there a before at all? We just don't know. But that doesn't mean we'll never know.

Scientists are exploring different ideas, different models of what might cause a tiny part of space to erupt in an expanding fireball to form the universe. They have some good ideas about what might have happened. Some of these ideas even suggest that such fireballs could happen within our own universe. Such a fireball in our own universe might possibly bring about the birth of a brand-new, separate universe, a universe "pinched off" from our own and completely inaccessible to us. That universe might eventually be full of galaxies, stars, planets, and life. Or the new universe might be completely different from the universe we know.

If such new universes really can be born, then an amazing possibility must be considered. Could it be that our own universe began just in this way, as a fireball in another universe, one completely separate from our own? And perhaps that universe began as a fireball in yet another separate universe, and so on. If this sounds familiar, you're right. It's turtles all the way down!

No one yet knows if these ideas are correct. Someday they may seem as unlikely as elephants on turtles. But they do point out how strange and unexpected our universe may be. And they show us just how much we still have to learn.

We live in a unique and amazing time. Just now, scientists are exploring questions that were once far beyond our grasp, and they're finding some answers to those questions. As always, each answer leads to ever deeper and more mysterious new questions. The whole universe, with all its possibilities, lies before us—an unknown ocean for us to explore. Like the newest generation of sea turtles, we are entering that ocean for the first time, swimming ahead—to where, we do not know. It makes sense along the way to learn what we can about this new home we all share. How did we get here? Where are we going? What *is* the universe, anyway?

While we ask, while we poke and prod and strive to discover the depth and breadth of this new ocean, off in the distance the sea turtle swims on. Here's hoping that as we ask, as we explore, as we learn, we save a space for creatures like the sea turtle, who have, through millions of years of their own evolution, come upon a simpler, though no less elegant, path.